To Bind Up
Their Wounds

To Bind Up
Their Wounds

Best Wishes

HW Trueblood

H. Ward Trueblood M.D.

Library of Congress Control Number: 2008904021
ISBN: Hardcover   978-1-4363-3977-3
                     Softcover   978-1-4363-3976-6

To order additional copies of this book, contact:
Xlibris Corporation
1-888-795-4274
www.Xlibris.com
Orders@Xlibris.com
49099

Contents

Dedication

For making sacrifices greater than we have the right to ask, this book is dedicated to our men and women serving in wartime.

"Deciding to remember, and what to remember, is how we decide who we are." These are Robert Pinsky's words, and they strike me as being the perfect introduction to Ward Trueblood's account, through poetry, of his life. Ward's choice to express himself in poems reflects his respect for the challenging and revelatory nature of poetry. "Poetry teaches grace," Ward said recently, and he has shown himself to be an appreciative pupil. He remembers the Iowa prairie, time spent with his father, a harrowing experience in Vietnam, his career as a surgeon, his travels, his family, his decision to retire from the practice of medicine. But he goes deeper, and allows us to see much more: the imprint on his boyhood of a neighbor's tragedy, his father's unfailing patience, his mother's death, the deeply buried wounds of Vietnam that come back to haunt him, the exhaustion and sadness that accompany his father's aging, the extreme tension of a surgeon's life, the terrible suffering of patients, the up-close and daily confrontation with death. Ward does not shy from exploring the dark, but he also expresses his joys: gardening and grandchildren, the blessing of a long and happy marriage, his love for his family and for the perfection of nature, his adventures, and his empathy for patients. It has been my deep pleasure to help him gather these poems and offer them to a larger audience. What Ward Trueblood has decided to record in poems is nothing less than the truth of his life, his work, and his heart.

MaryLee McNeal
March, 2008

Beginnings

Waveland Cemetery

The stories are there
behind each of the tombstones;
stories of sacrifice for principle;
stories of community, shared work, and prayer,
of a six-Percheron team on a single moldboard
to make one cut in the virgin prairie.

Great-Grandfather Smith
as a boy watched a defeated Napoleon
retreat from Russia;
he left Germany for Iowa and a religious belief
that war was wrong.

Great grandfather Crew
like all pioneer farmers
had a specialty craft carpentry
(his handmade set of maple planes sits on my shelf).
Others were blacksmiths, horse trainers, midwives;
each took their family to Iowa for better land.

The farmer on the open prairie
was tied to nature's vicissitudes:
windstorm, blizzard, flood, drought, grasshoppers, and illness.
They knew with a certainty and humble acceptance
they were not in control,
yet lived with awe and gratitude.

Grandfather Sam, as we all have since,
married a strong woman.
Sam brought his own strengths,
has been a model for each who followed,
taught by example: "Fall not out with a friend for a trifle;
                    find humor in life;
                    listen well to others."

The first hominid began in a similar grassland
in East Africa six million years ago.
Our cycle continues;
the grasses keep flowering.

What we leave is intangible:
a model of how to love
and a faith in the next generation.

My Wise Mother

At age six, World War II was in its last year.
While Dad was in a field hospital crossing France and Germany,
I would sit like a big boy and listen with Mom to the nightly news.
Despite the newspapers having graphic photos of dead soldiers,
army censorship proscribed Dad telling us where his unit was,
but he included in letters a description of local statues.
Mom would check reference books and show his location.
Most of the statues were war heroes.
I told Mom I wanted to be a soldier and have a statue, too.
She found me a statue of Louis Pasteur.

Autumn Tragedy

My childhood street was lined on both sides with giant elms.
Each November, great piles of leaves were raked into the streets.

How peaceful and safe it seemed,
to sit in a pile up to the neck
as the wind blew warm,
nestled in the womb of autumn.

A young driver on a noon spree did not see
the blond head above the golden leaves.

Bucky was the widow's only child;
no one ever said, perhaps he was her grandchild.
He was her whole life.

Her scream of anguish when she saw
his limp body still echoes in my memory;
a horrible, primordial wail, the sound of all breath and life
being forcefully extracted from somewhere beneath the sternum.

We never saw Mrs. Small outside her house again.

Growing Up With A Country Doctor

Some boys know their fathers
from fishing trips, ball games, duck blinds.

For me it was evening house calls,
hospital rounds, or a Sunday trip to the office.

As a child I sat on his lap to steer on dirt roads,
listening to Abbott and Costello or the Cubs.

We'd wait in the car while someone calmed the dogs.
A kitchen door was the main entrance,

where on a makeshift front room bed
we found grandpa asleep with sick grandma.
"Do you breathe better sitting up?"
The stethoscope in his ears was better than x-ray.

By college I could serve as his lab tech.
Uncle Charlie had diabetes so we'd check the urine for sugar.

Later as a medical student I did exams, scrubbed on surgery.
Night calls becoming a new fact of life,
shaking me: "We must go."
For this man to call,
he must be near death.

All he had heard was fever and belly pain.
We picked up the microscope and kit,
found the farmhouse porch lit.

The patient lay unmoving, belly rigid,
urine bile positive, white count shifted.
A daytime hearse/nighttime ambulance summoned.

IVs running, the surgeon was called;
all three met at the city operating room,
the ruptured gall bladder removed.

That summer, a young woman with metastatic cancer stopped me short:
"Am I going to die?"

They don't teach you in medical school what to feel or say
but I learned it at the bedside with a master.

Careworn

Sadness seeped into the emptiness
like morning fog coming off wet hay,
enveloping first the rusted John Deere
then the unpainted barn.

The look from nineteen months in a war zone hospital was returning,
the look of a man with all illusion stripped away.
When fatigue and pressure overpower, all masquerade was pushed aside.

My sisters and I knew the look, knew not to speak.
We rubbed his feet and combed his hair,
our mother played the piano while his warmth slowly returned.

The sudden death of his partner in 1948
coupled with the mass retirement of the towns' war-exhausted older docs
cast my father into an open ocean of needy patients.

Medical crises let loose the towns' inhibitions.
They came to the door during dinner, called many times each night,
found him in his garden retreat on Thursday afternoon.
The due dates of pregnant women controlled our family life.

He was a good doctor because he cared; because he cared, he worried.
He made concern an art form his patients could feel.
It eased their pain.

He was welcomed at the side door on home visits,
knew what room grandma would be in,
raided the drug cabinet for dangerous home remedies and outdated medicines.

His great strength was recognizing
both emotional and physical illness,
and treating both miseries just the same.

News of a patient having marital problems
would elicit a phone call.
Then he'd wear his other hat, as counselor and friend.

Humility made him a better healer:
"I want you to see a specialist" was a mantra.

The old sadness grew with retirement and loss of being needed,
then became bottomless with the death,
after six decades, of his wife and lover.

The silo and root cellar are empty, the pump handle gone,
the stories of the caring old country doctor
are but fables or pictographs on a cave wall.

Waveland

*"You are a child of the universe . . .
no doubt the universe is unfolding
as it should."*

Old St. Paul's Church, Baltimore, 1692
Max Ehrmann

I stand by my Mother's grave;
grass hasn't yet covered the dirt.
Dad and I read aloud
her beloved Desiderata.
The stone already bears his name.

The April wind makes it hard to stand.
The one tree in sight: a gnarly juniper
with broken limbs and many trunks.
The next stone south, sandstone, leans windward,
the inscription almost gone,
Great-Grandmother Lydia 1830-1895.

North lies Grandmother Effie 1867-1969
who told stories of the first turning of the prairie sod.

Twenty feet down through rich black soil lies
sandstone from an inland sea in the Pleistocene.

This place has the feel of a wilderness mountain top,
no comfort enticing me to stay for long.

I know with certainty my mother is not here—
just her frail bones.
Her spirit lives unconfined,
far too powerful to simply disappear.

Eternity is not remote;
I sense it in the leaden sky,
the 100-year-old peony on Lydia's grave,
this small remnant of unplowed Iowa prairie,
the courage of this fine old man beside me.

Dad at 99

Out in Iowa—
first snow come and gone,
leaves turned, all but disappeared—
survives a shed where a homestead once stood.

The fence line looks forgotten;
posts hang free of the ground, held
by a few remaining wires, anchored
to an ancient Osage Orange tree.

Oh tree, small and gnarly,
part dead, part alive,
somehow you hold your fruit
the long leafless winter.

Tell us what you know
of work, life, loneliness.

A Sense of Place

Aunt Ethel at 102 years would close her eyes
and paint a word story of her childhood farmyard.

My sister can do the same for the farmyard
of our wartime summer with Grandma.

In my dreams fifty years later
the action recurs in the childhood back yard.

One side: a perennial flower garden
where my sister was married,
where every year the catbird found a favorite bush.

Over the back fence, a magical thoroughfare;
a fifteen-foot-wide grassy alley where neighbors burned their leaves,
the back way from campus to country roads,
shortcut to see Bobby or Mousie or Moose,
play kick the can and hide and seek.

When visitors dropped by, the backyard became a summer parlor.
I traced its contour 500 times with summer mowing;
in winter it became a preserve of snow and bird feeders.

When I returned from Vietnam, the yard was a sanctuary of safety.
The dogs had moved on, but the catbird and wren were still there.

Now it was time for me to have my children,
and their own place of dreams.

Goodbyes

His emotion always made it hard:
mid-sentence change of subject,
long pauses, an abrupt turn to go,
never *I love you, too.*

Now his dementia is housed
in an overly-efficient machine
that won't quit.

He looks up, chin briefly off his chest.
I have been reading to him for three days;
a whiff of recognition crosses his face.

I imagine his inner voice:
Oh dear, still alive.
This most awkward and prolonged goodbye.

The Open Wound

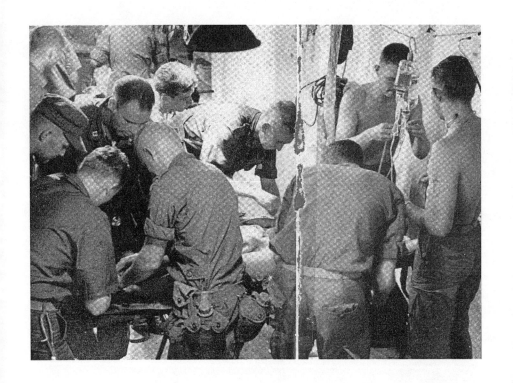

Nine Time Zones From Hell

We lived that year near the triage tent:
body bags dumped outside the entrance,
air turned rancid from wet fatigues,
sweat, mud, blood, and vomit.

Hand grenades clunked on the floor while disrobing,
amid calls for morphine, saline, and the chaplain,
while more helicopters circled to land.

Sounds and smells and visions of another world.

Given no transition to home,
no debriefing, no understanding,
we left one by one,
separated from the only ones who knew.

Thirty-five years later, I find
myself weeping, uncontrollably weeping.

I returned to the arms of those dearest to me
with a wound I did not know I had, buried deep inside.

A Bag of Memories

It's just a bag of old letters, collecting dust.
With every move it's treated like family ashes,
placed in the top back corner of the closet.
Seeing it, I divert my eyes.

I did not think I was wounded
that long year in Da Nang.
The hospital was blown up the night before I arrived.
We were fired on and shelled
and yet physical danger was trivial
compared to the men in the jungle.

I never shot or killed,
but the wounded died in my hands.
I cut off hundreds of mangled legs,
unzipped so many body bags.

Opening a present last Christmas,
a book on the battle of the la Drang Valley—
one look at the graphic cover flooded me with memories.
I lost it before my family.

I am haunted.
When I close my eyes I still see the wounded,
some so massively injured I could not even start to save them,
others requiring up to one hundred units of blood.

And yet during that year in Da Nang I never broke down;
the adrenalin—the need before me—
gave me a single focus.

The daily letters in that bag are a journal of trauma.
Something in me knows I must reread them.

I so dread the loss of control.

> *"Dear Nancy August 10, 1965 C Med Da Nang*
> *How I miss you----------today 40 casualties-------"*

So Sorry—Vietnam

From a helicopter
full of wounded Marines
she hands me her limp baby.

Breathing hard, rounded chest, blue skin,
diagnosis: congenital heart defect and failure.

A Marine is screaming—
they only do that when their brains
are low on oxygen from blood loss.

I am no heart expert
but the closest she can find.
No time for x-ray and EKG.

I give her a tiny dose of digitalis.
The baby dies instantly in my hands.

I give the baby
back to her mother.
She does not cry;
Vietnam is crying.

We came to this country to help.
The American persona: "Give a hand."
The Hippocratic Oath: "First do no harm."

Late at night, after all the work,
I recalculate many times the dose.
That same night, in Washington,
Johnson orders in 200,000 more troops.

It takes a mature physician
and such wise leadership
to know when to treat.

By late 1965 we knew we couldn't cure her.
The goodness of the American heart
was reduced to a body count
of enemy dead.

America was crying.

Comrade of the Open Wound

A Christmas card today
from an old friend.
No, more, he was my comrade.

A married guy with a Texas wisdom
irreverent and fresh enough
that no one was offended
by his straight talk.

I wrote him each year after Vietnam.
After years of cards from his wife,
I grew weary. We lost the trail.

We had lived 12 months in the same tent,
even shared a foxhole a few nights, and
the horror of what we saw each day.

I was drafted out of surgery training,
insecure of my competence,
but he, my anesthesia colleague,
could spot a cardiac tamponade across the room.

As the days and weeks and months passed by,
the body-thumping sound of incoming Hueys
meant for us the endless work of putting together
the fragile remnants of another 18-year-old marine.

I haven't seen Lloyd in 35 years.
Still, if I have a tough case,
I imagine him across from me,
his coffee and cigarettes nearby,
his tension-breaking presence,
looking with me into the open wound.

Sixty Four Years of Wars, But It Seems Longer

41 years ago I sat in a rain-blown two-man tent in Da Nang, the same tent used by the 3rd Marine Division in 1943. A stream of muddy water ran across the back corner, my cot perched on a plywood platform to keep me from sinking into the mire. Each night, only a letter and a picture pulled me out of despair. The wounded Marines I cared for have blurred into a collage of gaping wounds, fragments of legs lying backwards on the belly, some boys with agonal breathing, black with burns, gray brain tissue on their helmets, or sucking dark holes in their chests. When we learned they were wounded in the same valley as the platoon 2 days ago and the platoon 2 months ago, every doctor and corpsman and chaplain in the triage tent knew with overwhelming certitude we were in a war we could not win. It took Washington another 9 years to stop sending more. Fast-forward to Baghdad in 2007.

Forty Years Under
The Lights

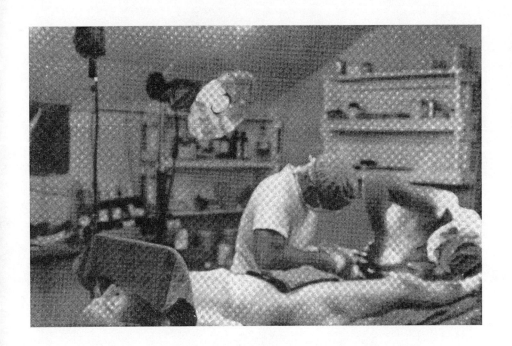

A Fortunate Man

We all have unexpected gifts.
I found such a gem;
rather, it found me.

It was always there, like an affectionate hound
pushing its nose into my life.

My mother had the wisdom
to let me and my sisters touch
take home, and respectfully bury
a freshly-dead squirrel from the road.

Later, I carelessly shot a swallow
with my older cousin's BB gun.
The harm I caused broke my heart.

World War II changed our lives.
Not knowing where my father was,
only that he was helping wounded soldiers.

By ten I was accompanying on house calls
and knew it was an honor to be asked.

That part of me,
the caring part,
grew out of those times,
grew into me
and made all the difference.

The Thin Line

Cross it:
instead of helping, you cause harm.

During seven years of post-graduate training,
a central theme is *walk it, but not too closely*;
when to cut, what's the risk, the worst case, how close.
As a career unfolds, each crossing
into the dark beyond is vivid memory.

As a third-year student,
I watched in horror as my professor crossed the narrow line.
He lacked both skill and ego strength to ask for help.
I learned more than if the care had succeeded.
Three years later, I crossed it,
in the jungle that was Vietnam.
I have crossed far too often.

All of us who stay in the arena
must make a truce with our own failures
yet go on, each time wiser.

Set Under Authority

For the farmer
  so the surgeon

Seeds germinate
  wounds heal

Rains come
  bleeding stops

Soil like human tissue
  will respond to caring hands

Neither farmer nor doctor have complete control
  only long hours of hard work
    and a daily glimpse of what is real.

Morning Clinic

There were 21 patients in clinic today,
some who delayed necessary surgery and
some who demanded surgery too risky or unneeded.
We listen to what is real for them and keep it simple.

The first patient is a barmaid
with breast augmentation pushing over the top,
a diamond navel stud
and the most insignificant anal skin tag.

An urgent side trip to the trauma bay—
a young football player with an open leg fracture.
He can't know what his doctors know about how his life has changed
as he breezes with a pretty nurse to cover his anxiety.
(A flashback, Da Nang—two Marines in ICU
fresh with bilateral amputations, making light of who is shorter.)

Melvin is preoperative, lives in a drug
rehabilitation unit and is very fidgety today.
He asks to pray over his surgeon's hands.
How do you say no?

Rita knew she had cancer going into the first operation;
now she must be told there is more.
More surgery
followed by radiation and chemotherapy.

This will be her third visit, yet there is
a kind of intimacy; in this business,
the most personal questions are asked.
Cancer has a way of sidestepping all pretence.

Long divorced at 62—
vodka and cigarettes push the time clock up.
On past visits we learn another side to her aloneness:
a troubled granddaughter finds her "too boring;"
the trailer court owner is threatening her treasured flowerbed.

How surprising to see her now reading
ancient Greek philosophy.
With grace, she brushes aside the bad news
like a pesky fly—"Well, let's get started."

Change

Kal has become an institutional project:
two trips to the O.R.,
back for two stents,
now experimental chemotherapy.

Every intern on monthly rotation knows him.
Early in his illness, his anxiety made him pesky.
At times—week after week—
he would live in his camper on the back lot,
be seen daily in the clinic waiting room or cafeteria.

He was in his prime in the 60's,
Gestalt therapy or Feldenkrais
but never a family.

Now he is slowly dying of GB cancer.
We are his family,
his connection to life and meaning.

We all note the changes:
his face is thinning, turning yellow,
his eyebrows more shaggy and white.

While he still entertains us with jokes,
he is also more prone to show his gratitude.

The biggest change is his acceptance,
his ease with the inevitable.

So many are destined to end up floating alone,
frightened at sea in the dark.

When we can no longer be a ship with a light for him,
we can still be the voice of a friend over the water.

The Face of Cancer

devoid of vigor
eyes set back
cheeks hollow
gums pale

the look, a mix of
pleading, knowing, fear,
no longer the clean shave
or concern for dress

would I recognize all this
had I not first seen the scan?

after all these years,
no need to itemize the signs

The Tragedy of Denial

He came into the ER last night with a mosaic of self-inflicted low back burns:
the hot water bottle took his mind off the deep pain.

Below his small, intelligent, and frightened eyes
sprang a neglected gray beard.

His teeth were black or absent,
the fingers stained yellow,

his nails extended an inch beyond the tips,
and the radial pulse bespoke anemia.

He spoke of unemployment, moving home with his mother, depression,
and insomnia treated with the "logical" drug, more Bud.

His jeans were in stand-alone condition and topped off
by unwashed jockeys streaked with blood.

The stigmata of alcohol abuse called out of
facial skin made ruddy and swollen.

Two years ago he saw a doc for the bloody stool,
knowing at some level that this was bad news, and failed to follow up.

We didn't need the CT scan or scope and biopsy
to diagnose rectal cancer with sacral metastasis.

Who could judge his two year walkabout
when our president has denied failure in Iraq for four years?

Decisions

Alex* died of starvation,
a solo trip into Alaska wilderness.
Mysteries remain, why
he cut himself off from family.
He went north to prove himself,
to live alone on his own skills.
There came a fateful day,
strong enough to walk out,
yet for unknown reasons—ego, pride, lack of connection—
he missed his opportunity, lost his life.

Olga died of gastric hemorrhage.
At 75, depressed and alone,
she had lost contact with her family.
After bleeding 9 pints in 48 hours,
she would not be persuaded to accept
desperately-needed surgery.
No friends or family to call for encouragement,
she returned to her isolated apartment, fleeing
into her own Alaskan wilderness.
A taxi driver brought her back in shock—
she too had passed a fateful window,
missed a chance to ask for help,
died from lack of love.

Nora will die of cancer of the pancreas.
The waiting room filled with supportive family and friends.
"We have not been able to cure her, but have given her a year."
The decision was eased with such support.
Her daughters stayed with her each night;
she left the hospital, jaundice gone in a week.
This extended family, built on years of caring,
in turn would produce a year of life.
Her end will not come alone or with regret.

---

*   *Into The Wild* by Jon Krakauer

It Is Written

In Memory of Mary Ann Beswick

When all that can be done has been done,
each soul
will be cast upon the ocean for a final journey.

This will be a time of heavy seas
and night will become void of all light.

Beloved family and loved ones
cannot help us hold to the floating beam.

Their voices will grow more muffled
as from a distant wave.

It is written
each will cross over to a sacred place.

All who love us will follow
at unknown times,

and in its own mysterious way,
memory will work its wonders.

One-Way Road

In a dream I climb a mountain road,
pushing hard until the way becomes steep.
I turn to go back, and see many others
are backed up, to do the same.
Down the mountain the road is swept away,
traffic stopped, refreshing what I already knew:
accept what can't be changed and move on.

Resilience

Daniel was in for a post-op visit.
He is a physician
but as a patient had fought for his life,
overcoming paraplegia from meningitis,
complicated by a perforated colon,
sepsis, respiratory failure,
a month in ICU, two months in rehab,
now relearning to walk.

As we talked, I saw
a tiny inchworm
moving up his sleeve.

We sat down together, watching in silence
at the metaphor of recovery
as it crossed his palm.

Moments

Perhaps the biggest tragedy
of dying young,
whether war,
a bad decision,
or some natural cause,
is all those missed moments.

Those flashes of insight
awareness
stillness
knowing:
this moment is of value,
this moment is real;
together, they make a life.

Some moments are universal,
some are individual:
      the magic by a bluebird's flight
      the perfect scale of a canyon wren
      the feel of the warm autumn wind
      the beauty of a face transformed by a smile
      the hug of your adult children
      the nod of a near stranger you had the knowledge to help.

Best of all, waking up at night,
passing your arm around the beloved,
always the same way: under her arm,
over her breasts,
and feeling her pull your arm close.
All worry and pain and clamor become insignificant.

Poetry teaches grace;
time teaches us gratitude.
To not live for these moments
would be to die young.

Grace

I wake up at 3 AM
to hear the great horned owls
who who whoo-who who,
and then the answering call:
who's awake, me too.
The call is not used solely for night hunting;
it's the way they stay in touch.

This night I am touched with gratitude,
an unexpected gentle breeze,
aware of the beautiful hillside
shared with the owls.
I think of my wife of thirty years beside me,
a touch and she reflexively comes closer.

During the day I am too busy to hear and feel;
maybe that is what wakes me up:
the need for thankfulness
pushing through sleep.

I become aware of my mother,
can see her smile.
Do departed souls form a force of good
touching us when we're too busy?
Sleep returns before I hear the answer.

Loosening The Bonds

Life's Work

We visited his wooded Vermont farm,
where years of work had sucked him dry.
Walking through the old barn,

we pictured the winter work
where the family made maple syrup
the last 100 years.

At first it saddened me to think
of a life measured only by cords of wood,
gallons of distilled syrup each season.

As time passes,
the early sadness for Mr. Orvis
is replaced by a certain envy.

He spent his life outdoors in a beautiful place,
made a worthy product,
and worked with his whole family.

Each of us writes a story in the end,
perhaps not measured by cords and gallons,
but by what and how we have loved and lived.

No More Going Back

The plan at age 67 was to dabble
around the soft edges of medicine,
being useful, assisting, mentoring,
drifting well away from responsibility.

Then came the wake-up case, assisting
a young colleague at the limit of his skill,
the patient bleeding, the cancer not out,
surgery past the point of retreat,
fast-moving towards an operating room death.

The forty good years under the light
were rapidly pushed aside,
replaced by a premonition of purgatory.

Placing stitches in the back of the portal vein,
the inner voice is loud and clear:
"Don't get in this dilemma again.
You are not a soldier home from war,
asking, out of boredom, for another tour."

I was lucky and knew it.

Looking Back

No nagging
No wishing *if only*
No thought of *I should have.*

Yes, I could still respond
to the 1 AM tense voice of the ER doc:
"A guy in shock and a tender belly."

But I used up some essential reserve;
the desire is gone.
It vanished as quickly and silently
as the moon slips behind a cloud.

From those first days on the ward,
I loved it more than myself—
the power of knowing
what was going on deep to the belly wall.

There is nothing so magnificent and ecstatic
as saving a life, and so addicting.
But such a terrible, demanding master.

It was a sojourn into another world,
almost a lifetime.

Now I live to play on the floor
with little Patrick and Owen and Katie
and show my children
the love I have for them
a generation late.

Solstice

There is a sadness, an impersonal
coldness to the summer campus.

The bronze Rodin faces
tell nothing praiseworthy.

The new stone- and-glass buildings
grow in number each year
and emanate more aloofness.

Even the palm trees
have become more artificial.

The curious international visitors
study quotations on the chapel wall,

thus missing what hope the silence holds.

Winter Wheat

There is a variable, wavy line of latitude
north of which wheat is planted in the fall.

Determined by a short growing season,
the farmer may plant only Hard Red and thus produce the bread of life.

Indecision chills me like a cold wind on a sunny winter day.
Open ground may either freeze or thaw.

I have retired before, only to return
to this 50-year love affair with medicine.

This work has always been risky, a
narrow path between cure and complication.
Somehow it seemed easier in a former life.

Hard Red Winter Wheat, to be grown in Iowa, must be
planted in the fall: too early risks the Hessian fly larvae,
too late and winter storms prevent germination.

There is a timing in a surgeon's life,
those cold mornings when the birds begin to flock,
an Indian summer of vigor left for a new and different harvest.

Unburdened

I pause by my medical library
known intimately for forty years,
and turn instead to a biography.
The rest of my life is turning, too.

The essence learned from the practice
of medicine is not forgotten.
The beauty of the human spirit,
the amazing healing power of nature.

That part of my life soon ends;
I am waking refreshed and free.

Gone the annoying chirp of the pager
on every family outing,
nights, weekends, constantly
overriding any other agenda.

Perhaps there is a limited amount
of responsibility one can hold
in a lifetime—if you care.

I delayed the change earlier,
thinking it a dishonor to the insight gained
at the bedside of the sick.

But now my office closes.
Old patients will object.
I will miss their gratitude—that daily gift.
I will miss being needed,
but the shadow side was always
the potential of a poor outcome.

My new life mission: being grandpa or papa,
a different kind of fix-it man.

"Homeward Bound"

Simon and Garfunkel
"for a poet and a one-man band"

Holding forth in the antechamber of the restrooms,
singing our story to whomever would listen,
while outside, ten-foot snowdrifts define the summit rest stop.

Seventy-something, sad eyes and a Willy Nelson beard,
accompanied by a cheap guitar and music stand
proclaiming, "Re-elect nobody."

He has the look of a Vietnam Veteran, a painful story,
a clean-cut small-town kid who learned to kill and mutilate,
ruined by drugs and alcohol, now living the only war he can, alone.

A mortar trajectory to the north and south of his concert hall
lies an empty, snowbound, and foreboding wilderness.

A reminder, lest we forget,
of our destiny and insignificance.

Healing

Perspective

Surrounded by desert canyon majesty, overlooked by the vast landscape, a pinyon pine and juniper grow side by side, close enough for branches to brush together in the wind. In sandy soil beneath, the lizard tracks a form of Asian calligraphy, and the ants seem preoccupied by some unspoken authority. The rocks are a subdued pink and cream and purple. Westerly storms blow through and are gone in an hour. Underneath the sage, bunch grass and flowers are respectfully spaced. The wind seems always in the distance. Pristine soft air expands the night sky. Visitors to this land speak infrequently and in hushed cathedral voices. As the trees age, the roots grow more intertwined. One is oddly asymmetrical and the other scarred by lighting. In time they lose limbs, hold the soil, provide shade and fruit for new seedlings. Woodpeckers, jays, and chipmunks live on and spread their seed. How perfectly the two have added peace and beauty to this place.

Uncompahgre Plateau

We ride dirt trails between golden aspens
made more beautiful by the occasional green
of spruce and pine.
There is no sound but tires on fallen leaves.
The only wind is in the shimmering aspen.

We lose the trail without anxiety—
this day, a precious interlude before winter.

We lie in silence after lunch,
cirrus clouds suggesting change,
as does the rainbow around the sun.

Pinyon jays fly in groups of fifty,
there is new snow on the La Sals,
yet summer lingers below in the Unaweep Valley.

One needs these times, almost a geologic cut
from all consuming work.
I sense my harvest is in:
our marriage holds passion,
the children grown mature and lovely.
For the first time I visualize my work ending;
the season has changed.

At its base this young plateau,
unerodible Precambrian rock,
diverted the ancestral Colorado River,
withstood untold winters.

Our life through all its changes,
a truly demanding ride
testing what bedrock we possess.

Only In Cazadero

The four of us biking Sunday morning foggy roads,
the long and scenic route to Fort Ross on the coast—
flat tire stalled near the only country store in miles.

The couple appeared out of the cold redwood hills
in a pickup with windows down, a male shirtless driver.
We sipped hot coffee and wondered at the power of whiskey.
She had not an ounce of fat or sense of shyness,
somewhere between thirty and sixty and impossible to ignore.

On her shoulder rode Manny the King.
The strut of the trainer and rooster were the same.
"Do you want to see this rooster play the piano?
He'll be on Letterman within a year."

Egged on by a tin of worms
Manny the King went into a flurry,
pecking and clawing the little piano.
Music? No, but another memorable ride.

Sonora Time

Warm breezes come in periodic breaths.
Sage and creosote bush sway,
ocotillo seems choreographed
to a different rhythm.
Aged saguaro just stand and observe.

Note the Curve-billed Thrasher's song
is liquid and refreshing.
The Gila Woodpecker entertains
by hanging upside down,
deep in the shade
of a comfortable 90 degrees.

Even in retirement, one can take
a lesson from the desert
in midday slow down.

Tomorrow we leave
this pace and peace
for artificial deadlines,
phones ringing, late in traffic.

We'll call it life.

Palapa Time

There is a time of day—a time of life—
on a Mexican beach.

It would not happen if all life
was fair and free of pain and sorrow,
if every bird outing discovered
the song of the Canyon Wren.

Near the evening, after a day under a palapa,
the sun will slide into the ocean haze,
turn orange, and the eye can see into
a different time.

Upon hearing the rhythm of the waves
in tune with forces of the stars,
the hurts and oversights that keep us awake
seem insignificant.

There is a lovely assurance that the setting sun,
like yesterday and the day before,
will backlight this same isolated island.

What forces are these
that draw us to this place
where nature is so raw and exposed?

Is it an accident
that the enduring love for family
and the things we cherish
are modeled in some primordial way
on the faithful rhythm of night and day,
tide and wave?

Lessons From The Garden

Look at this volunteer tomato plant
growing from last year's compost heap.
What surprising courage and vigor,
daring to add chaos to the neat rows.

Then there is the aged Rambling Rose
that tries to grow beneath the Hydrangea.
(Silly me, to impose my will.)
I cut and hack it back to a leafless stump,
yet back it comes again and again
sometimes a foot away, a sort of lateral arabesque.

Will the volunteer seed breed true,
or award me with a new flavor?
Who will the grownup individual become?

As for the rose,
it's like the family argument over thorny issues:
the aim is just containment.

Goodbye Garden

How odd that I could leave it
so suddenly, so completely, so lightly,
like a casual acquaintance on a bus.

The story is older than nine generations of farmers.
It was my father's hobby, the big jobs he let me do,
the special spade his father used, smell of his work shirt
that I could pick out of a line-up of smells 60 years later.

I did not understand the magnetic pull of the garden
that grew slowly, relentlessly, with the growing tension of my work.

Each season so alive, saying "look at me,"
each a new dance with an old lover. What good
therapy for the sleepless worried mind:
planning crop rotation, when to prune or pick.

Even pulling weeds while sitting on the moist spring soil,
soft and non-resistant: hypnotizing and uniquely satisfying.

Oh, the beauty and quiet of the garden
can stand alone as its own reward.

Yet there was a point when each new plant or tree
crossed a line, and like too big a family,
joy slipped into pressure.

Now while work and worries drop away to a more simple life, I remain
one of the mortals left to have tasted a delicate 10-minute-fresh ear of corn.

Temple of Sinawava

The Virgin River
arises like magic.
A simple crack in a 2000-foot cliff—
source of creation to the Piute.

Red rock canyons filled by
sun, and sage and rabbit bush,
pinyon pine, coyote and the Kingbird.

Names convey the remoteness and mystery:
Paunsaugunt Plateau, Fifty Mile Bench,
Cedar Mesa, The Cockscomb,
Hackberry Canyon, Escalante River.

To a forty-year girlfriend
and her stressed, balding beau;
southern Utah is life.
Call it a yearly pilgrimage.

By day we drive
two-rutted range roads.
An abandoned corral marks the source,
another magical canyon hike.

By night we wrap together,
sheltered only by a transparent roof tent.
Moonless, the stars are indescribable.
The wind flaps the tent,
making us feel more safe and together.

Our skin bronzed by sun and dirt,
each day filled with simple chores,
coffee and oatmeal by camp stove,
evening wine toasting the sunset.

The desert has again bestowed on us
simplicity, quiet, and healing.

Mystery

Two old people who now look alike,
maybe, but we have our secret:

what we see the world does not.

Expressive wrinkles around your eyes
that slightly questioning look that only I know
tightening lips clearly holding back a smile
now familiar sideshow of the missing sunglasses
your addicting nighttime touch and smell
your familiar drooping breasts easing thought
of soft flab around my waist.

You somehow still see the strong,
good-looking man of 40 years ago,
and to me, you are drop-dead gorgeous.

Return

"There is a day
when the road neither
comes nor goes, and the way
is not a way but a place."
Wendell Berry

Near a hilly country road sits
a sagging barn, unfit for cow and hay.

Choked with weed and cobwebs,
home to sparrows and mice,
the hay baler lies stalled, tires flat,
the last bale yet undelivered.

I imagine a downpour and lightning,
last year or five years ago,
the equipment hurriedly stored.

This hilly beautiful land
no longer a rewarding farm—
the hay no longer cut,
no cows to tend.

The owner has taken a "town" job
yet the setting and memory pull.
The land drifts as do we
towards where we began.

March Morning

The wind blows music on the window.
The tree bounces,
straining to move across the hill.
Light dances over the water on the deck.
I breathe
in stillness
having made my song,
bounced and danced,
still blessed with health and time.

Acknowledgment

Thanks first and foremost to my wife Nancy, who has been my soulmate and support from the draft notice to the present, and to my wonderful children, their spouses, and my five grandchildren. Thanks to my parents who had the wisdom to set a tone by living and writing their life stories, and to my two sisters and all eight generations of Quaker ancestors in this country who lived lives of merit and principle.

This book would not have been possible without my editor, MaryLee McNeal, who felt the message and tone of the poetry had value. Together we understood that the anticipated readership was my family, friends, students, and any who understood our common journey.

Thanks especially to my poetry writing group which grew out of a 1996 *Stanford Continuing Education*, poetry workshop led by Jen Richter, a Stegner Fellow and Jones Lecturer. We continue to submit our work monthly for critique and support. Thanks to MaryLee, Nancy, Rick, Narda, Marian, Nelly, Lisa, and Chris.